S. Bahozde's (Saladdin Ahmed) Elsewhereness antipoetry actualizes its stated marching orders via forceful dialectical serial logic and keen humor (hilarity, really). This book is an "act of attacking the unimaginability of a better world."

The Bikonian-Fanonian bursts of anti-poetics, their counter-measures break past the givens to model how such—proper name, place, political calculus—engender and resist, repel and authorize cunning sequences of anti-capitalist trespass. An (anti-) poetics that playfully negates its aesthetic medium of refusal and choice, all the while setting its sights on its key mark: encroaching nihilism in the face of brutal displacement.

S. Bahozde's work dismantles claims in favor of negations clearing forth space for open-ended, future liberatory claims. Its poetry as propositional logic's meditations on completion, works, and absence is shudderingly smart. This is poetry as food fueling revolutionary exilic work.

— **Jeremy Matthew Glick**, Professor, African Diasporic Literature and Modern Drama, Hunter College English Department, City University of New York, author of *The Black Radical Tragic*

A voice speaks here which is at once profoundly Kurdish and cosmopolitan. While tracing the melancholy of the spaces of exile, its loneliness and longing, Bahozde takes the reader into spaces where the disillusionment with history does not lead to nihilism. Here the brevity of aphorism tackles the tangled metaphysics of absence and existence. Here is a foreignness that take us away from "pickled banalities" and disturbs our complacent belonging to places, nations, and histories.

— **Rohit Dalvi**, professor of philosophy, Brock University, author of *Deleuze and Guattari Explained*

This is a passionate and bold set of works that range over topics and concerns widely with an almost febrile intensity. Bahozde's poetic negations of "normalcy" gain their strength both from rich philosophical insights and from a searching, provocative imagination. Even when set in moments of apparent languor, they have an evident, restless energy.

— **Gaurav Majumdar**, Whitman College; author, *Illegitimate Freedom: Informality in Modernist Literature*, 1900-1940

Elsewhereness
Antipoetry

S. Bahozde

Daraja Press

Published by
Daraja Press
https://darajapress.com

ISBN: 978-1-998309-28-3 (print)
ISBN: 978-1-998309-30-6 (epub)

Book and cover design by Kate McDonnell

Library and Archives Canada Cataloguing in Publication
Title: Elsewhereness : antipoetry / S. Bahozde.
Names: Ahmed, Saladdin, 1972- author
Identifiers: Canadiana 20240473108 | ISBN 9781998309283 (softcover)
Subjects: LCGFT: Poetry.
Classification: LCC PS8601.H64 E47 2024 | DDC C811/.6—dc23

To those who belong nowhere and everywhere.

Contents

About this Volume

I am grateful to everyone at Daraja Press for their essential role in creating this book. My gratitude goes especially to the founder and publisher of Daraja Press, Firoze Manji, for placing his confidence in the project and working hard to ensure its publication in a timely manner. My sincere thanks to the reviewers as well for their endorsement of the project.

In the preliminary stage of the process, Firoze Manji asked about the main idea/thrust of the manuscript, and I wrote a response to him. Later, on Firoze's kind suggestion, I decided to use that piece as the basis for an introduction. However, all my attempts to make it more fitting as an introduction ended up rationalizing the project, which is something I want to avoid. I prefer to stand aside as the author and have the texts speak for themselves. That said, the following, which is the verbatim piece from the book proposal, could help readers who may be curious to know what they are about to get themselves into as they start reading this book.

The manuscript is a collection of creative texts written by an immigrant at the border of languages, geographies, and histories. The reading experience is meant to enhance transgeographic potentialities of intersubjectivity across generations and continents. The texts were written over several years in response to the various forms of displacement, estrangement, and exile that are systematically imposed on the exploited majority. The book is a response to the nihilism that has been normalized following the supposed end of history propagated by the ideologues of exploitative privilege and oppressive power.

As a Bikonian Fanonian, in my philosophical and theoretical works, I address the same issue in terms of problematization, analysis, and critique. In this manuscript, however, the goal is not pedagogical; rather, it is to provoke other dimensions of creativity and imagination in the face of a totalitarian climate where we have been told repeatedly that there is no alternative to the existing order, that the prevalent state of affairs represents the best possible world, that the dreamability of a better world was merely communist propaganda, that the Black

Consciousness ran its course in world history and the movement is over. The book as a whole attempts to challenge the regime of truth in which imagining an alternative world is not possible, so the main idea is emancipatory negativity.

The main thrust that runs through all the texts is negation. I mean the negation of what is perceived as "normal" through de-normalizing nuanced belief structures and unspoken social rules. To that end, the texts aim at the dominant modes of perception through an artistic deconstruction of the given, the real, the beautiful, and the good. As a writer, my means of resistance against domination and tools of deconstruction of hegemony must be invented within the framework of language. The book contains various attempts toward that objective, with each text creating a new point of departure for denormalizing, deconstructing, and negating.

Each text is linked with the rest through a harmony of mood and style. Put differently, each (dialectical) tension created within each textual point (or moment) is situated in what some surrealists used to call the marvelous. But I am not a surrealist. To determine what constitutes the marvelous, I cannot claim to have a theory or even a hypothetical set of literary criteria. I can only invite you to read the texts. I am confident that the experience will embody the uniqueness of each hermeneutical rapture and the book as a harmonious whole.

The book's overall harmony emerges from articulating the poetics of solidarity within a universal/ist movement of resistance. Breaking conventions creatively, the negative articulation itself is perceivable universally. We are not islands, but we are made to feel and act as if we were isolated islands. Like you in Daraja Press, I believe we could and should bridge. Borders are the worst means of identity construction. As a communist and post-nihilist citizen of the world, I call for collective violations of the sanctity of borders through international solidarity with those who cross borders motivated by hope for a world without any form of violence, including poverty, which continues to be systematically produced and imposed on the marginalized.

Strictly speaking, the book is not poetry. It is, in fact, anti-poetry. Like Adorno, I do not think poetry is possible in our world. I am even somewhat disturbed by the idea that one could write poetry. However, I find it equally impossible to go on without writing anything against such an unpoetic reality. Over the years, there have been moments of the crystallization of what can be called the poetic negation of the unpoetic reality. The idea, then, is to share something creative in order to inspire something creative by the reader. It is to disturb the mentality and the language that continually internalize hopelessness and naturalize nihilism. It is, at the same time, to radically reject the industry of false hope. The book is the act of attacking the unimaginability of a better world. Instead of stating all or any of these claims, the book conducts negations. It negates the dullness of linguistic figures and, through this, the banality of everydayness. My hope is that the reading experience will help produce moments and spaces of solidarity across and despite the social and political borders that have been violently imposed on us. In a gloomy age as ours, the prospect of moments and spaces for solidarity may be invaluable on individual, intersubjective, and communal levels.

This is not poetry.

A World to Pedal into Being

Let us bike away

to another land, a different land,

where poetry is possible,

where poets don't eat so much shit,

where having a state is not necessary for living with dignity,

where people do not die because of myths.

———～～———

Let us bike and reclaim the ability to dream.

Living dreamlessly is very much like falling into a gym

where people unstuff themselves of bad poetry.

Or, let us bike back to the times we did not have,

the worlds we could not build,

the revolutions we lost,

and the losses we forgot.

Somehow, if we stop, we fall.

We fell and dropped the season we had sculpted together
    on the border between dreams.

In the margins of great empty goals, we managed to
    sleep with the garden,

sketch a return of the lost gazes,

and gaze at the traces of nameless migrants.

The city was hard to dislike, and it is harder to miss.

Yet, there, we managed to bike a few years away
    while seasons were still four,

spring was still an official season despite poets
    and their fellow mass murderers.

———～～———

I say, let us bike to another land,

away from soldiers, teachers, doctors, and other poetically
    disabled people,

where boredom is a legitimate reason for revolution,

where every face is worth more than all the flags in history,

where poets are taught to farm potatoes,

where people can be interesting even after they speak,

where we won't need to keep biking to avoid small talk
    and other fatalities of everydayness.

I say let us bike away before we give existential disappointment
    a chance to turn us into some sort of inductive asses.

As we bike away, I will recite the biography of the river
    that ran through the unmissable city,

and maybe you will tell me the story of the clouds
    that kept appearing and disappearing as we were busy
    shopping for another reason to skip another small talk.

Behind the pines, I had a vision of a path, two bikes,
    and a world without poets and French restaurants.

The following day, I heard people speaking of Jesus as I was
    thinking about going to China.

A week later, I dreamt the Republic had banned all blue bikes
    and cancelled all the seasons of the year.

I was stuck in an elevator where Jesus and Mohammad were arguing
    about the best kabab place in the city.

Friends had gathered in someone's backyard to discuss socialism
    and the difference between whisky and scotch.

Let us just bike away and never sit in a class, a trench, or any other
    factory of fascists,

to a world where poetry is possible but not necessary,

where gods have better means of communication than donkeys
    and fucken ghosts,

where life after 30 does not feel like the same news report repeated
    eternally,

where nobody needs to listen to imams, hunters, and barbers.

<center>~~~</center>

Let us bike and remember to remember that a small talk is
    the first symptom of artificial intelligence.

Let us bike away from this land where clouds are forced
    to carry passports,

where trees are named after men who wore beaver skin
    on their heads,

where rivers are forced to commit genocide,

and authors of sacred books are not required to get a degree
    in science.

The year of the last spring season, city squares froze to death.

Since then, inductive asses have taken full control over the fate
    of clouds, sunsets, and artificial deontology.

One of us headed to the east in search of the lost season.

The other stayed nearby in search of a café that might allow
    another love story.

One of us searched for the traceless migrants discovering
    how unpoetic the sea is.

The other was determined to strip metaphysics of absurdity
    only to discover nothing.

Then, we switched tasks.

Something was missing in everything.

There remains a season to reinvent,

a world to pedal into being.

Another Home

It is time to pack a few memories, wrap the dreamed horizons, unframe the gray painting along with Che's burned face staring into the so-called living room for a winter and a half, and invent another road in search of another home.

Once the bureaucrats bring their machetes to the table to behead language in daylight blessed by all the sacred books that had been penned to eternalize murder poetically, it is time to lose another so-called home, follow the traces of the northern wind's childhood, and walk away.

When the wrinkles of bourgeois boredom are regularly accumulated in pension plans, an unlived life is delayed for an unlivable age; when the dreadful grass is guarded by a depressed dog trained to racialize homo sapiens; when gravy-covered youth is meticulously prepared for Thanksgiving and the Butchers' Day, it is time to leave your home that is not your home and be on your way.

In the distance that separates a dimming memory from the fascist gaze of the patriotic teacher, the spotless desks from the depressing small talk that precedes every damn meeting, loss from forgetfulness, the rain from landing, programmed laughter from fanatic moderation, perfect informality from formal rejection, a French restaurant from mechanically reproduced gestures of romance, spirituality from falafel, divine revelations from a descending elevator, the holy scripture from dry-cleaned faces, diversity from the capitalist engineering of liberty, liberty from the butchered animal's last lost gaze;

in the distance that separates *The Wretched of the Earth* from lecture halls, the "send" button from the expired horizon of a moron's dream, the barbed wires of freedom from the ability to dance with closed eyes, the closing door of the elevator from the unoccupied Wall Street, the mandatory smile of a colleague from the Yazidi mass graves;

in that distance, *the small blackfish* may swim away guided by neither divinities nor philosophies but by *the sound of water's feet* walking towards *another birth*, a birth without colonial permits, international sanctions, official addresses, or cover letters.

When banality becomes a privilege, mass-produced expressions a celebrated sign of civility, happiness an anti-depression pill to be taken before a date with instrumental rationality, health an empty white room;

when gardening becomes a Nazi hobby to kill spaces that have survived time, blue cheese a culturally qualified member of a panel chaired by a refurbished jihadi, Gilgamesh a guest of honor in a reality show;

when poetry becomes emotional prostitution, creative writing an ingredient in brown cookies, Walter Benjamin's face a visa stamp, the Arab Spring carbonated water, Nirvana a near-death experience of collective sweating in a gas chamber designed to liquidate depression;

when the meaning of life becomes a learning objective of a course taught by a white Californian who had found the path to her inner emptiness and the secret of mindfulness while devouring a cheap but authentic Indian meal;

when the hippies with pension plans become indistinguishable from Brownshirts with leather hats;

when the men who would sell their mothers into slavery for a free bagel set out to determine why you do not deserve the honor of being their colleague;

when punching death-driven smiley faces becomes a reoccurring daydream;

it is *the beginning of a cold season* and time to pack a few memories, trash everything else, and leave in search of another corner where you will be able to commit the act of existing.

Going to China

People around here talk about talking to God.

There are no sidewalks, but nobody seems to notice.

The amount of positivity is depressing.

It is the totalitarianism of bourgeois hollowness.

The fall has not arrived yet.

The coldness has never left the faces.

Empty gazes keep crossing empty gazes.

Evenings come to block nights.

They speak of prophets

and bite on food with a lot of emotions

You are thinking of going to China

and getting a cat

Nothing moves,

like a photo titled Boredom on a museum wall,

like the gaze of a frozen face,

or an empty chair unpoetically placed among other empty chairs

---

People are fanatically sticking to the center of emptiness,

walled by piles of packaged meat, processed speech, and dried smiles,

chained to the messianic promise of an illiterate messenger,

they spare their enthusiasm for the next stop of the train
   they missed long ago.

One child is too few, and two are too many.

This year's stupidity is emptiness mixed with spices and sugar.

The instructions say to keep it at room temperature.

But at room temperature mushrooms grew and new eggs of pure
  hallucination hatched.

Then, they spoke of speaking to spooky immortals.

In Siberia, one could master Marxism and eat rye bread with a
  shaman.

In July, one could walk to China,

camp in inner Mongolia for a night and turn the mistakes of history
  into brandy,

and on the way back to autumn tie a blue ribbon around the Tao.

Tell your protagonist to tell them that Africa is not a village.

Tell them to stop saying "I love India!" as if India were a cat.

Haven't you met tons of gendarmes of knowledge who believe in this
  or that holy book's promise of universal justice?

Anyway, if I were God, I would commit suicide out of sheer shame.

A scholar was not sorry for the genocides but apologized for saying
  it was a cold day.

I used to hear everything's music.

Walls, buildings, roads, stones, clouds, rivers, and trees,
  all had their own music.

Deontologically speaking, a raccoon is way more moral
  than an ethics teacher.

Down on the street, a woman was singing, "Kant, Kant, Kant.
  Who the fuck is Kant?"

The Chinese Emperor called the Brits savages.

A while later, the Brits sent dead frogs to all the corners of the planet.

Some anarchists had a thing for the Queen's hats.

The Stalinists in Baku fell for a mustached Duce

while his Sultan was conflicted between the spell of curtains
and the call from the phallic.

I hate all flags equally,

except for my country's flag,

which I hate the most.

Exile is where you are not.

Behind the pines, there was nothing to photograph.

Over there, where machines had forgotten about your fingerprint,

where you had forgotten how to blend into the regiment,

where aging hollow men and women were busy canning youth,

at the crossroad between slavery and the Wild West,

where only a willow could have reminded you of yourself melodically.

Then, we slept with the wind after a night-long laughter.

We laughed at the way things are.

Ever since, when we meet, we laugh at the way things are
for a long time.

Then, we sleep in whatever way we end up covered partly by longing
and lifted by forgetfulness.

Like a child's drawing, people are stuck in their lines and angles,

doomed by the tendency to see the world geometrically.

Despite its odd verticality, the human caged itself in a deadly
horizontality.

To make up for the lost dimensions, people pour artificial colors
and flavors on their plane of boring existence.

Like a child's drawing, there is always a lost dimension in
being a human.

Every place is just one end of a line and one point in a circle.

The odd verticality has not pushed back the planarian vision.

Like a child's drawing, the human project is clearly ridiculous
even to humanity.

Places belong to stones.
Eternity is shapeless.
For it is an illusion.
Exile feels cold and empty.
To the exile, all places are mere paths,
paths to and from the heart of the stone.

Yellow Exiles

January collects the exile's shattered fragments,

elegantly placing eternity on a journey toward the first longing.

Northern nights slip through a melodic gaze at the border between
fading times

Every day is a journey's second day, something the present
fails to catch.

Longing holds curvy paths and sharp memories together.

Longing for belonging is exile formed on a cold day,

eternally rewinding the week's journey only to end in absence.

———

Turn to thoughts that have texture when the evening comes.

Remember that someone was here before the beginning of the
cold season!

Other years will be gone in no time while the place is still sored by
nostalgia, numbed by letters.

X stands for an unwitnessed drop of rain, and Y for the shadows
with blurry edges.

Exiles are yellow.

Later, you will see that only the exile could make home attainable.

Long before the dwellers die though, the exile leaves.

The Foreigner and Communism

I am a foreigner.

You, on the other hand, have a life.

There is no need to apologize for forgetting the forgettables.

I take it upon myself to recall insignificant details until they become immortal.

―――――

Every evening, I lock the door on loneliness.

I weave the morning using ancient threads of memory and fresh light rays that come all the way to pass through the window.

All windows suffer from insomnia.

―――――

Sometimes, the brain forgets how to fall asleep for days in a row.

Some nights the dreaming brain makes a familiar face promise not to disappear once eyes are opened.

―――――

I am only a foreigner taking refuge in a dreamless land.

The chair in my room is multilingual, but the curtain is deaf.

―――――

I wonder whether those who are trained to speak so casually about nothing could be trained to appreciate nothingness.

I overthink words until a word multiplies like an organ growing on the wall of a cave or its shade.

Words start saying things other than what they are meant to say.

I do not take pride in writing a book that takes a lifetime or reading an age's worth of books.

I take pride in surviving a two-minute interaction with the glazed faces and programmed characters of the age.

One night, just after I brought back loneliness to turn it in,

as I was hanging up memories to dry up for the long winters ahead,

a decade-long story reached its conclusion in the trash.

When the wound happens, it feels like nothing ... maybe a small irritation but not a big deal at all.

Then, the pain grows and grows until it reaches a point where it cannot grow anymore without smashing the wounded into pieces.

Yet pain grows even more and still a little more.

Then, it starts to recede for a minute only to return a minute later interrogating the wounded for the missed minute.

Eventually, it will allow life to live.

It becomes a scar on the face of the wounded existence.

An animal's gaze at universal injustice or a child's broken stare may remind one of the wound, being wounded, being a wound, and wounded beings.

I was a foreigner.

Then, I decided to go to foreign lands to make my foreignness somewhat fitting in terms of being unfit.

I am at home with my foreignness, but to this day my foreignness is not at home.

Every March I reexamine mechanical reproducibility of saudade.

At the border:
    – where are you heading, Sir?
    – To the other side.

To the other side of the Phenomenology of Spirit!

On borders between vanities, there is only so much dialectic one could conceal in a suitcase full of forgetfulness.

There is always another side of foreignness.

To be foreign is to be outside.
Outside polished identities, sacred flags, and pickled banalities.

———⁓———

We, foreigners, may fall into or jump out of the urban noise at
    any moment,

but our foreignness is a dancing being with a life of its own.

It takes us on long walks in the rain and makes us enjoy random
    moments and places.

We spend our lives waiting for great historical events.

Our foreignness, however, refuses to wait idly for history to happen.

It picks fights with mortals and immortals.

It protests both routine and the lack thereof.

It approaches the world syllogistically but articulates its horizons
    poetically.

It aims at geometrically structured propositions but cannot stand
    right angles.

Foreignness, in the court of history, is accountable for both creating
    and killing every deity.

———⁓———

My foreignness, for instance, has an issue with the god who not only
    claims the name for himself but also insists on using the most
    primitive of means of communication to send what is allegedly
    the most vital of all messages to humanity.

My foreignness does not find donkeys to be the wisest choice for an
    omniscient being, even if that being does not have a degree in
    mass communication.

Donkeys themselves have nothing to do with such embarrassing
    metaphysics or the epistemic failure of the divine regime
    defended by herds of philosophers.

———⁓———

Theologians are officially licensed abusers.

Philosophers, being denied a mandate, apply self-molesting while
brain-yogurting their fellow citizens.

I mean to be polite, but every day my foreignness offends at least
a fascist, a theologian, a philosopher, or one who is all three
at the same time.

Foreignness is linked to our wild origin, both positively and
negatively.

The alarmed look in a foreigner's eyes is the same as the look in the
eyes of a hopelessly lost or imminently trapped animal.

Disturbing but nothing is more truthful than an animal's gaze.

The suffering that had been meticulously hidden behind walls
of smiles can be betrayed in a moment by the eye.

One is always at work to distract others from seeing what is not
meant to be seen

But the foreigner is more obsessed with words, searching for the
one that says everything.

On behalf of the hopeless ones, in my room, I put all gods on trial
and announce full independence.

On the celebration day, December 26, Mao's birthday,
I raise my teacup and condemn the divine will.

The foreigner wants to say only what does not sound foreign.

But he is only interested in what is foreign

The foreign makes the foreigner go further into exile in exile in exile.

I do not want to see you anymore because I no longer want to be
casual, and the non-casual has already left.

What a deep embarrassment; I apologize for seeing you as a
poetic being,

for projecting foreignness on what is otherwise fatally casual, pathologically healthy.

There is no point in saying goodbye to those I will not remember anyway or those I will remember anyway.

Someone said, "But hate is a strong word, and I said, "I hate what you've just said."

I also hate half-Marxists and their mass-produced excuses, Smithian and their privatized brain cells, sentimentalists and their fanatic centralism, optimists and their fidelity to boredom, golf players and their bad sense of color, poets and their chronical phoniness, humanitarians and their egoistically modified modesty, librarians and their intellectual coma, butlers and their sincere bad-faith, mass murderers and their English attitude, soldiers and their hollow spouses, yoga teachers and their constipated happiness, former revolutionaries and their inseparable glass jars, managers and their metallic glaze, diplomats and their ontologically bogus lifestyles, border guards and their poorly plagiarized claims to loyalty. I hate them all and hate those who do not hate them.

On a strictly personal level, those whom I hate the most are those who would put the same smile on their faces even if I were Mussolini.

No worries. it is just me. I overthink things. After all, I am a foreigner.

You, on the other hand, have no time for the foreign in the world. You have a life, so to speak.

I dream of a corner as a home and a glimpse of homeliness.

Nonetheless, I am most attracted to the most foreign woman, the loneliest of all possible lovers.

Other than the woman of my dreams there is no metaphysics for me.

———

I rather stop seeing you not because of the poetics of equality but for the equally distributed poetics.

After all, I am a foreign communist.

I will disappear from your ensured life and artificially flavored evenings, not for the sake of my communist dream but for the sake of the distribution of poetics.

Your home is my abyss.

The life that created the glazes in my colleagues' eyes scares me more than any concentration camp.

Your kindness offends the little bit of humanity in which I still have faith.

My path is majestically empty, long, and cold.

If I fail, I fail majestically.

Your busy life is filled with processed intentions and gray expressions in need of constant treatment.

Erase me from your list of semi-lovers, quasi-friends, ontologically disabled believers, artificially gentrified theologians, and existentially dead preachers.

I don't hate you. I hate crowded social deserts, passionless worlds of shallow Daseins, the psychotic positivity of bourgeois hipsters, leashed forms of existence, mental molesting, textbooks, and yoga mats.

You have an amusing life full of activities to fend off depression, anxiety, and suicidal thoughts.

I, on the other hand, am a communist.

On the Other Side of the Pine[1]

I am a worker with a black mask turning to the sun.

The sun goes down while I am still searching for another space
    for dreaming.

For dreaming, these cities need to be freed from all the garbage.

Garbage has covered my history and sieged my world.

My world will rise and bury all the garbage except for the last bell.

The last bell will be rung once and then turned into a bowl for water.

Water will suffice for life.

For life, we do not need holy men, sacred books, golden ornaments,
    and bloody crescents.

———

I am a worker armed with a will, a hope, and a spade.

A spade is all I need for bringing down, cleaning, and building,

building a world in which the temples will be the streets.

The streets will be the city's poetry for my spade.

My spade will have already buried all their bells except for one.

One bell is all I need to announce the end of their history.

The end of their history will be the beginning of my world.

My world will not need poetry for it will be poetic.

Poetic it will be the blackness of its nights and the sparkle of the sun.

The sun and I will rise tomorrow for a world without nightmares,
    without garbage.

———

I am a worker who is not welcome anywhere in the holy land
    of holy men.

Holy men took my world and gave me a nightmare.

1. Inspired by the image available at https://tinyurl.com/mskphyw9

A nightmare is the world in which I am made to freely sell my life.

My life has paid for everything by sweat and blood.

Sweat and blood for their gods and goons, mansions and minarets, brothels and bethels, flags and tags, malls and walls.

Walls kept out my comrades, paralyzed my dreams, and imprisoned my horizon.

My horizon though will shine again once I smash these walls.

Walls belong to their world.

Their world is my hell.

———

I am a masked worker armed with my body, spade, will, and hope, walking towards the other side of the pines.

On the other side of the pines, poetry is possible, and life alone is sacred.

Sacred or not, on the other side of this nightmare, I will bury their histories along with their swords of horror.

Horror is to wait for another life, another promised heaven, and another slap on the demarcated being.

Being there, on the other side of the pines, not the other side of death, is the single purpose of my single life.

My single life will smell like the pines, and the pines will suffice for poetry.

For poetry to be possible again, I am walking towards a revolution,

a revolution that has neither nationality nor color, neither gods nor prophets, neither borders nor states, neither judges nor prisons.

Prisons were the holy lands, and prisoners were all those who dared to dream of another world.

Another world is breathing behind my black mask, a world without nightmares, without garbage.

The Oppressive

A bureaucrat calls you "sir!"

Fascist leaders are incapable of smiling.

Every classroom is a chair's nightmare.

Every stone, tree, hill, street, corner, house, cloud

Every silence, texture, scent, or movement has its own music.

In every being, a smile persists.

Even the most tormented sufferers, in their hearts, carry a smile.

Except for bureaucrats and fascists.

The Duce, the Führer, the Supreme Leader, the Caliph, and their armies of bureaucrats,

along with their dogs, are drained, dried, wrapped in culture, and preserved for the age of nation-states.

When that age comes, holy piss is sparkled on them,

all that has been conserved by sanctified cultures will come after life in every corner of the world.

Paths unfold us. Through these paths once walked the forgotten ones. How many times must have they sent their lonely gazes into the endless space enveloped by darkness? How many times did their lonely hearts speed up in excitement at the sight of something different before slowing down again in the sadness of the cold passage of time?

The Mistake vs. The Falsehood

Every exiled is extra evidence of the attainability of home.

Every religion is extra proof for primordial schizophrenia.

Kobane – Events

Four little children walked down the street
    and ceased to see the ruins as ruins.

They were merely walking down the street.

God was too insensitive to notice the event or admire a window.

A flower was emerging from the crack of a rock.

Only one of the children noticed it.

The flower shaped so many childhood thoughts without words.

God missed the flower and the thoughts.

A cloud was passing over the town.

One of the children noticed its shadow moving over the fallen houses
    and looked up to see a cloud moving eastward.

He saw clouds as clouds, roads as roads, houses as houses.

He was more sensible than all the gods and poets in human history.

A wound can become the center of your being.

Or your way of feeling streets, houses, and clouds.

A wound makes you feel your physicality better.

If you listen closely, all things have their music.

Years and many more clouds passed

The children went their different ways

There was no trace of the flower

That particular cloud was not in anyone's memory

One rainy day, old friends gathered in a café and drank black tea.

Outside the window of the cafè people were just walking.

It looked like a painting, but it was just a new window of a new café
    in an old city on a bloody border.

Near the main road to the west, there was a graveyard for
    those who died liberating the city from God's armies
    over the years and centuries.

Completed Texts

1. Only when you look for yourself in yourself, can you miss yourself completely.

2. When you listen to me, I just want to listen to your silence, your thoughts.

3. In you, I see the you who has not been heard yet even by you.

4. Every morning, the path takes me to the following week, hoping that you will be there to meet up just once, and the paths together go straight into the heart of the horizon where nothingness is absolute, eternal, and immediate.

5. I come from borders and hate where I come from, so whatever you do, do not leave me wandering on the borders.

6. You have no idea how easy it is, for you, to make the world the best possible one for the world's worst possible dweller.

7. Maybe it is just me, but the way things look is not the way things look.

8. Every othering is a delay in everything. In the end, life is postponed indefinitely.

9. What offends me is not that you do not see who I am but that you will see me when others will recognize me. Now you might say my problem is that I am arrogant. Then, you will say my problem was that I was too modest.

10. Those who expect nothing and hope for nothing can only be saddened by the memory of the present.

11. All memories are demented memories.

12. The present, when not seen as a second edition of yesterday or a preface for tomorrow is majestical even when melancholic.

13. Fear of the new makes one a captive of sequences of dead moments, rendering the present impossible.

14. Most people become shadows of four years of their lives, missing every coming and going train while replaying the same clips of themselves supposedly waiting for a train. It is no wonder most people are fatally boring and can only hang out with their "best friends."

15. I do not wait for too long. If I wait for you for too long, it means I was gone long ago.

16. Health is a bourgeois myth.

17. There is nothing more lethal for the intellect than light, especially steady light.

18. Those who are used to too much light are intolerant of themselves, or maybe they have intolerable selves.

19. Everything has some sadness in it, so the world is not a strange place for the sad ones.

20. I think I prefer your absence because when you are present, you are not present.

21. She who can be present when she is here is someone the presence of whose absence is felt sharply when she is not here.

22. Parents are not entitled to brag about caring for their child because the child in the most literal and ontological sense is their fault.

23. What is most shocking about stupidity is its limitlessness.

24. A genius explains things so well that the utterance is perceived as a truism.

25. An idiot perceives a genius utterance as a statement of the obvious.

26. Happiness is intellectually offensive and psychologically depressive, but it is morally ok for those who might be undergoing rehabilitation from religion or even other, that is, less serious, forms of addiction.

27. Here is the story in one line: You tried to bring me down to the trash. I tried to lift you off from the trash. We both failed.

28. If you try for it, then it is not love. If it is not love, then you are being cruel to yourself, and later, when the farce is over, it will take a lot to eventually be able to reconcile with yourself.

29. You attribute meaning to what is otherwise meaningless and deny all that is meaningful meaning. Then, you complain about the absurdity of the world. You are the source of absurdities.

30. The moment another book is written, the list of unwritten books becomes longer.

31. Among things for which I could never forgive myself was subjecting myself to idle talk.

32. I have been going in the opposite direction for so long that I am now surrounded by infinitely long paths each of which beautifully merges into the horizon.

33. If you compromise about small things, you will not be able to tell what is not small.

34. If you compromise once, you will compromise a thousand times.

35. The ability to fall is far more important than the ability to stand, that is, if we are talking about human beings.

36. Those who fall and stand up with a little more determination will end up taking the most out of every day wherever there may be.

37. What I have is nothing to you, and what you have is nothing to me, so a relationship would not last.

38. It is not that I don't believe you; rather, I think you don't believe you. So, if I follow your wishes and desires, both of us will end up losing faith in me.

Absence – An Anthology

1. Absence is the only true poetic concept, which is why it must be protected from poetry.

2. Absence is a mask you put on the face of the present and forget to remove.

3. Absence is a wish searching for its form in the distance between the present moment and its death.

4. Absence is repetition fleeing linear notions of time, endlessly smashing itself onto the frontiers of space.

5. Absence is a temporospatial experience made of blocks of silence framed by stillness and separated by rapture.

6. Absence proves that the only spatial principle we can be certain of in all times is distance.

7. Absence is a projected biography of distance.

8. Absence is the psychic resurfacing of unlived closeness that has been suppressed.

9. Absence is the spatial experience of distance.

10. Absence is the unconscious unfolding of a melancholic yearning, frustration hidden under utopia.

11. Absence is a look sent to an emptiness that is tragically real.

12. Absence is an impulsive force that pushes the intangible aspects of your existence toward nothingness without interfering with history or spatiality.

13. Absence is everyone's first experience of hopelessness while hope is everyone's first introduction to absence.

14. Absence is disappearance enduring its own fragile occurrence to hopelessly undo the entanglement of time and space.

15. Absence is a claim on reality that is too weak to die, too lacking to endure, and too specific to surrender to the ultimate emptiness.

16. Absence is the reversed act of worlding or what puts the pseudo-action of waiting in motion.

17. Absence is the right to resignation exercised by those who refuse to act as right holders.

18. Absence is the instance of perfect fidelity, that is, fidelity for its own sake, or, fidelity to what is not, which amounts to the same thing.

19. Absence is perfect failure or, to be more precise, a perfectionist's ideal failure.

20. Absence is the determinate commitment to uniqueness when the latter translates into choosing nonexistence over banality.

21. Absence is to fail majestically in protest to a world without right options, or a commitment to failure when perfection is exiled from reality.

22. Absence is the only form of mental conspiracy plotted against the material limitations of the mind.

23. Absence is the disappearance of some appearance for which there is no real indication.

24. Absence is a hypothetical space for an illusion that is too real to whither away or a reality that is too unstable to exist!

25. Absence is multiple possibilities with mismatched roadmaps to reality.

26. Absence is the ultimate proof that the project of humanity is contingent on ongoing disturbances.

27. Absence is mathematics paralyzed by a bleeding memory.

28. Absence is a tender wound at the edge of forgetfulness, holding memory captive between being and nothingness, preventing you from moving in either direction.

29. Absence is a life shaped around stillness while leaking continuity.

30. Absence is an imaginary space invented by those whose lives consist of scattered exiles.

31. Absence is an assumed space that enfolds the existence of those whose everydayness is too colorless to be lived excitingly.

32. Absence is the dancing smoke at the heart of the stolen attention of a postponed life.

33. Absence is the refuge for a mind that escapes the wounding sharpness of exile.

34. Absence is the presence of an exiled being sensed by those whose existence are barely tolerated societally.

35. Absence is a space you imagine in order to escape those who are everywhere, and everywhere they consider you to be from elsewhere!

36. Absence is the fulfilment of a promise made by no one or the utterance of a statement in an unborn language.

37. Absence is the possibility of homeliness that is denied admission into reality.

38. Absence is emptiness at the moment when confusion takes place within a loneliness that has been hung up at the middle point between hope and frustration.

39. Absence is the nearness of the moment of arrival but without anyone to arrive, a perception without a perceived, an othered being who is bleeding its consciousness into elsewhereness.

40. Absence is an objectless event, a subjectless occurrence, and as such it endangers all phenomenological frames of reference. It is not that nothing takes place, but what takes place is nothing.

41. Absence is a supposed event that flees its metaphysics only to be experienced as the negative embodiment of eternity frozen at the present moment.

42. Absence is a motion pulled back by physics and fueled by the powerful otherness that is at the core of your falsely assumed essence.

43. Absence is the void when it hopelessly claims a space in reality.

44. Absence is the dual failure of recollection and forgetfulness.

45. Absence is a special black hole that swallows the subject's reality to replace it with a temporal hyperreality centered around subjective nihilism.

46. Absence is a tense moment of experiencing total void.

47. Absence is a dim perception of what is not at the expense of what will be.

48. Absence is memory being zeroed temporarily while you are in a state of daydreaming as if at the edge of existence returning an eternal gaze.

49. Absence is the proof that a human is an animal without an essence, that there is no such thing as human nature. A human is an animal that constantly wants to be what it is not. Humanity is both a potential project of suicide and a potential project of creation.

50. Absence is the wrong presence of someone or something in a mind that is unaware of the actual state of being.

51. Absence is a state in which memory commits itself to memory by negating the imposed boundaries of re-membering and forgetting.

52. Absence is the stubborn will that emerges from nowhere to magnificently challenge what the guardians of the oppressive reality like to call "natural law," "human nature," etc.

53. Absence is phenomenology invalidating itself while also negating every theory of validation within the conditions of experience.

54. Absence is the poetic taste of the tragic enveloping the reality of those who fail majestically.

55. Absence is absurdity turning against itself while painfully rendering rapture almost durable and almost locatable.

56. Absence is the resilience of the will to stillness against the suffocating power of the continued passage of time.

57. Absence is the banality of reality framed with the distance that separates a human life from the project of humanity.

58. Absence is the servitude that is undertaken by the memory of the exhausted exiled mind at a time of total hopelessness.

59. Absence is the ultimate fate of the real or a promise made by the possible but kept by the impossible.

60. Absence is the state of perceiving non-existence negatively, so it can only be when being as such becomes dubious.

61. Absence can only be where whenness is demolished or when whereness is demolished.

62. Absence is the virtual re-presentation of a single dimension dialectically negated to be transformed into an assumed multi-dimensional state. It occurs through a process of repetition powered by a state of repetition.

63. Absence's whatness is negative, so it can only take place as pure relationality. It is the only negating wager of hope against distance, departure, and mortality. It is human hopelessness in suspension.

64. Absence has perfect negation in common with hope. Put differently, absence is where re-presentation is. Likewise, hope is where hopelessness is.

65. Absence is thought's realization of its existential failure to account for time and space except as a disembodied entity falsely claimed outside all frames of significance.

66. Absence is a momentary vision of the self as a god committing suicide at the sight of reality.

67. Absence is the imminent and overwhelming totalization of elsewhereness.

68. Absence is exile repeatedly multiplying otherness thereby totalizing confusion as if thought commits itself to the impossible task of conceptualizing void.

69. Absence is the desperate desire to repeat what is not in order to escape what is.

70. Absence is the algebra of the repetition of what does not take place.

The End of an Age

Aside from being born, nothing is an accident.

What occurs sometime in an evening, on a rainy day,
near a mountain, makes pathways into turquoise memories
and melodies.

Names that come up in a November evening and defy all
forgetfulness may be evoked by the northern wind.

All other names will wither away along with engineered expressions
professionally distributed, quantified feelings carefully rationed,
borrowed emotions sincerely capitalized, and boring lives
painfully endured for the sake of pensions.

Divinities together with these tourist modes of existence will vanish.

All events come in pairs, except for recollections of melodies carried
by the northern wind.

The existential mistakes who were born on rainy days, those whose
namelessness travel through others' homelands, lives, and gray
window frames, will leave a scar in the face of the sun, a scar big
enough to frame every morning and every unanalyzable dream.

The lonely exile alone comes alone and leaves alone.

The exile is habituated by countless dreams of habitats.

In a fascist world, only fascists feel at home.

At home, the Gestapo agents and trainees persecute dreams.

A world in which socialism, not an afterlife paradise, is deemed too
utopic, is not worth knowing.

I reject homes and architectures, homelands and pedagogies, national
flags and ethics, states and metaphysics.

I denounce the real and the actual.

As the last communist, I salute persecuted dreams, silenced truths,
expelled hopes, marginalized horizons, and not-yet constructed
futures.

Photocopy

You, for once, were on time,
not a century too early to meet the first Bolsheviks,
or a split of a second too late to return the gaze of a shooting star.

No gaze has ever cut through these distances between
a spatial wound and a house,

A dream is placed in the absoluteness of a stone's existence
and a house, breaking engineers' chauvinistic rule of
not allowing the rain in.

You were never interested in the fossilized look of monarchs
who had a thing for nasty hats and brutish colors,
monarchs who mistook Caribbean islands for
German pancakes prepared for a royal breakfast.

Life was a situation you never got used to.

Every morning, you would dream of the shadow of snow
and the psychology of rain.

In the evenings, you would take poetry to the ER.

On your way home, you would burry divine will in an unmarked
grave and flush national honor down the sewage.

The garden is a refuge for the imaginary,

where the victims of everydayness regroup.

At sunset, you would poetically sentence justice to death.

The way the rain rains, you will happen.

You will happen the way only you can happen.

The Berlin Diaries were already 90 years old.

Exile is the human condition; home is merely a daydream in exile,
and the exile is a spatial wound, bleeding youth but with
endless fidelity to life.

After all, "I must live until I die. Mustn't I?"

The way the rain rains, you will happen.

You will happen to the world.

The Dog with an Office

History has always been quarantined, and
God keeps dying in the ambulance right after a wall is brought down
and before another is built.

Health is a bourgeois myth.

Happiness is a prescription for the upper class, and stupidity is one
of its side effects.

Those who rob everything tell those who are robbed: happiness is a
state of mind.

The students were anxious about the end of the world and selling
their future body into slavery to pay back for the services they
received in the death chambers.

Suffering from a severe deficiency of revolutionary anger, they
developed suicidal thoughts.

They were told, "grab a paper bag and breathe in it. It'll make you
feel better."

Did we establish that happiness is a mindless state?

Groups of inmates were assigned to fully trained counselors
equipped with proper AI technology and postmodern Gestapo
agents authorized to authorize torturers.

A fully licensed dog, in an office even John Stuart Mill did not have,
received inmates who had not yet discovered that misery too was
nothing but an emotion.

The revered expert in emotional support, however, could not
understand anything about the proletariat or the deadly effect
of the bourgeois everydayness.

He was just a dog doing his job of being a dog in a world run
by licensed hippies and other children of an intellectually
constipated God.

Saudade

Exile may be a nightmare or a trip stretching from youth to grave.

There is something poetic about remoteness and something remote about every evening walk along the river.

I blame the bourgeois gaze for the death of these rivers.

But nobody can be blamed for these dusty memories and deadly attacks of longing for what does not exist.

The home exile is the mother of all exiles.

Home is a daydream taking refuge in a garden or alongside a stranger walking from nowhere to nowhere,

a vaguely recollected dream that colors a lifetime, one day at a time,

a mythical creature devouring mythical futures quietly, steadily, and irrevocably,

a suppressed longing for pre-world times before one is born,

a transfigured desire for pre-history before gods are fabricated.

Behind a million mandatory smiles, in a remote corner of existence, the exile feels cold.

The Continuing Red Glory

The edges of presence are too sharp to be known all together.

The silence of this infinitely stretching road is unbearable.

The sheer awareness might permanently injure consciousness.

Not to be here is equally wounding to a memory already expelled
into the traceless.

If sound comes in diverse forms, silence is infinite.

Absence retains endless silences, each with a distinct tenderness,
a yearning for yearning, and, perhaps, a touch of clandestine
mourning.

The shiniest morning of the most vivid day of a life takes place
unnoticed.

With the passage of years, the memory only becomes brighter.

Every day, you are left with a little less ability to take on the sadness
that has increased a bit over the slightly growing distance
between one departure and another.

Longing for the times we did not have slowly sculpts windowness
at the heart of all barriers.

Nostalgia for worlds we could have built, paves the path to other
horizons.

The touch of every stone embodies the tenderness of silences
patiently forming the intimacy of this absolutely real world
in its magnificent godlessness.

From stones, the exile learns that sorrows erode, horizons crystalize,
the darkest of ages end gloriously.

Windowness

Hey you, exile! Your window stays up all night, every night.

But, no. Nobody actually said that. Nobody noticed or cared about your window or a stretch of silence that could last for five seasons or until counting fades or a season suddenly faints leaving you and your glorious utopia stranded with nowhereness.

The sight of the orphan window always shapely conscious of distances has the power to give void a texture smashing the sacred into pieces falling and vanishing faster than an owl's dropping in the middle of the night in the middle of nowhere.

Windowness is the invention of longing.

Do not believe those who claim windows are related to walls and doors.

In the birth of every window, there is a recognition of the metaphysics of distance.

Windows betray the unpoetic posture of buildings.

They betray an ancient fascination with elsewhereness.

They return the gaze of the exiles across ages and lands.

A single window can resist all the hopelessness in the world.

A window's testimony suffices to prove God's armies, states, classes, and constitutions guilty of crimes against humanity.

Absence as the Economy of Distance

The ruins of a house stood there pointing to crimes barely buried
   in the dust.

There was nothing but dust, around the murdered window, the
   streets, and the graveyard.

I just wanted to lie down and think about the emptiness that
   felt so heavy, the silence that was devouring the horizons
   of the present.

The air was full of absence.

In the dust, the presence of absence takes over.

A bird's dropping on the ruins of a temple has more claim on
   the dusty existence than the all the immortals together.

Every evening, I go for a walk to think about the genealogy of loss
   and the physics of absence.

To this emptiness I am so used.

Absence is noise except it cannot be sensed by any one sense;
   it stands there with nobody but sharply present.

It is silence knocking on the window or almost musically
   surrounding windowness.

Absence is the silence that ambushes you the moment
   you open or close a door.

It is the void that stimulates waiting,

 or the condition of experiencing distance

in a world eternally buried in dust and rearranged by storms.

The Political Economy of Honor

What is the point of shiny horizons if nobody arrives
from elsewhere?

If otherness is blocked or buried behind the walls of terror,
home is nothing but a prison, a stable.

These installed eyes are the concentration of intelligence
aiming to build a concentration camp for all.

Under the omnipresent gaze, only perversion will be secured,

Your Majesties and Honorables everywhere: if not for those
who step on your borders and sanctified flags, your nations
would be nothing but incest.

The Next October

For the besieged, all divinities and the conventions of justice are
not worth a pair of shoes.

Moving along the margins of silence, injured beings do not give a
shit about national pride, patriotic rubbish, aristocratic manners,
tenured butchers, or matryoshka prophets.

Home is a death camp for the annihilation of childhood.

When windows are tortured to confess and seasons are squeezed
to present birth certificates, some dreams will always find pages
to smuggle them to the other side of the barbarian age.

In a window's biography there is more to admire than all the walls
erected by the assassins of flight and prisoners of utopia.

In exile, everything turns grey, but stones keep pressing on the
dust of fallen ages while the dawn of a new age breaks through.

Let us dust our minds and awaken our windows to make sure that
we will not miss the arrival of the next October.

Otherness

From a distance, even this dull spleen of muted hours and days may
   sound like an ontological picnic decorated with sparking crystals
   from a thriving galaxy.

When other times are here, even one's present ability to attribute
   genuine depth to otherwise fatally shallow faces may be excused
   or even revered nostalgically, every walk along every river would
   be worth a million good novels.

Without packing anything from the contaminated land of the
   guardians of the reality, let us leave and refuse to arrive in
   cemeteries of time as time will not leave time for licensed
   protests, baptized symphonies, and groomed autumns.

Do not embark on patterns of boredom to bring what could
   never survive among stamped lives and petrified gazes.

The glazed eyes, programmed speeches, and gentrified colors
   of this endless hollowness will lower your blood pressure
   to the edge of nausea.

Insured lives are fatal for artistic taste and the ability to be wounded.

In the honor of the October dream, in the spirit of a migrating
   bird's single-purposeness, let us surrender to the power of
   eternal departure.

I can only fall in love with the path.

To hell with the tediousness of all locations and the social pendulum
   of death.

Let exile be absolute and eternal.

The African Present

In the first quarter of the 21st Century, just before what has become known as the second wave of fascism, biodigital archeologists recovered the following speech that is believed to date back to 150 years ago:

Stay where you are. We come to you. We love you where you are. You may come for a visit. You may transfer your money. You may keep digging for gold right where you are, but for God's sake just stay where you are. Nothing personal, but there is something about your presence that does not sit well with our way of enjoying life.

According to historians from the same team, the speech could have been delivered by an African delegate addressing Europeans. However, more recently, the archeologists retrieved another part of the same speech, which, in the historians' view, confirms beyond any doubt that it must have been by a European official addressing Africans and not the other way around:

We may find your presence unbearable. We may be compelled to drown you in the sea or sell you to mercenaries, missionaries, or jihadis, but remember we adore your culture. We will do everything to make sure that your culture is well represented, exhibited, adored, advertised, manufactured, and sold properly.

Negations

1

There was a world filled with unburied bodies, expelled refugees, and tanned tourists.

Billions did not have a handful, but a handful had billions.

No shortage of bullets, tanks, bombs, and soldiers, but water, food, and shelter were made scarce.

"I love Africa," a tourist said while his wife was putting sunscreen on his back.

> *Things will change.*
>
> *Things will not change.*
>
> *Change will change.*
>
> *And barbarism will be called barbarism.*

2

The misery will go on until death.

For the miserable ones, the only universal justice, the only hope not to hope in vain, is death.

Let us be reasonable, may be the oppressed deserve it,

Maybe it is meant to be this way, let us be reasonable.

> *Reason is not reasonable.*
>
> *This adjustable justice is guilty of cannibalism.*
>
> *Return martyrdom to the sender without a thank you note.*
>
> *Let us be realistic and do as Che said.*

3

On a cold February day, a professor with the glazed over eyes said:

this is the end of history and ideologies;

the east is under our control;

we have saved all Africa from revolution.

A student wearing a hat with a red star woven on it responded:

Fascists believe fascism is the end of history and ideologies.

But the sun will always rise, and it will rise from the east.

Africa will save us all.

4

In a gray classroom full of boredom and broken dreams,

as depressed students were unknowingly being turned into eternal inmates,

The rich spiritualist teacher confidently announced:

Happiness is a state of mind, but it takes absolute positivity, unconditional affirmation.

> *A student of historical materialism who had been running from work to make it to class, replied:*
>
> *Masturbation is a state of mind, Sir!*
>
> *Happiness is a state of life.*
>
> *Happiness is communism, and it takes absolute negativity, a revolution for the beautiful life.*

My Name is Bantu Steve Biko

I come from a racialized and banned Africa, walking toward an
    unchained and undivided Africa.

In my Africa, you do not need anyone's permission to believe
    in equality.

We have no place for vertical invaders and missionaries,
    or Churchills and Hitlers.

I may not know when an egalitarian world will come into being,
    but I know too well that this racial world must be rejected now.

I laugh when perversion claims civilizational superiority.

In my Africa, we do not trust pseudo-socialism or half-baked
    humanism.

If you are expelled for believing in equality, we call you a comrade.

Liberation does not need a passbook or a social security number.

Togetherness does not need spiritualism or alcoholism.

Freedom needs Africa.

Castes, classes, and races are barbarian inventions.

I stand with the untouchables, the cursed, the proletariat,
    marking the beginning of the egalitarian history.

Blackness is neither given nor denied.

It is obtained by rejecting the world of victims and masters.

To turn imposed identities upside down is to be Black.

Black thought is the negation of the mentality that has raced
    everyone to justify its apartheid everywhere.

The revolution for the undivided world takes off from Africa,

my Africa, where you do not need anyone's permission to
    believe in ubuntu.

In my Africa, we do not appreciate museums where booties
    of genocide are proudly exhibited.

We do not name streets and towns after mass murderers and looters.

We do not care about ethics textbooks written by slave owners
    and pedophiles.

In the languages of Bantu, the technology to colonize, destroy,
    enslave, and mass murder is not called civilization.

A world in which people cannot imagine an alternative needs
    revolution.

A reality that allows Sharpeville and banns dreams must be replaced.

In my world, Africa is appreciated for not advancing tools of
    mass murder.

In my revolution, everyone is welcome to unlearn apartheid,
    undo race, obtain Black Consciousness.

47

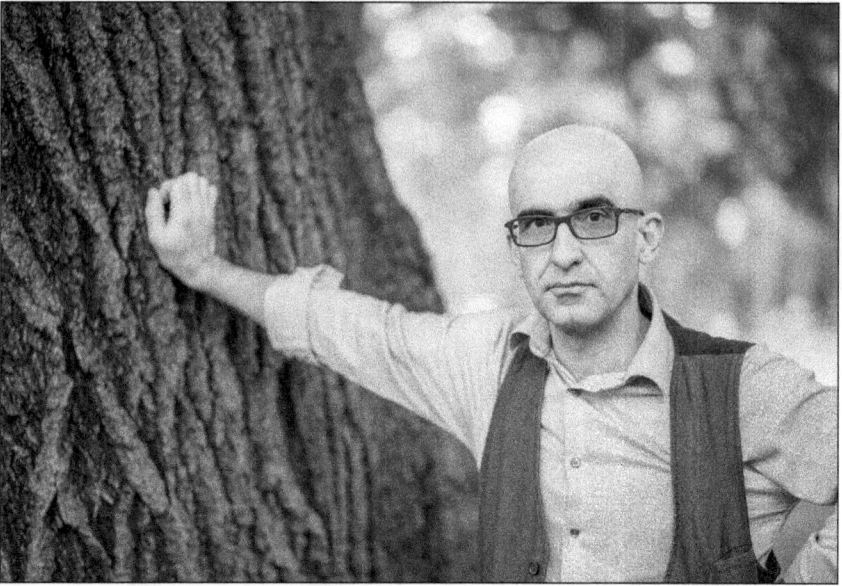

S. Bahozde, also known as Saladdin Ahmed, has also published *The Death of Home* (De Gruyter 2024), *Critical Theory from the Margins* (SUNY Press 2023), *Revolutionary Hope After Nihilism* (Bloomsbury 2022), *Totalitarian Space and the Destruction of Aura* (SUNY Press 2019), and *Fascism in the Middle East* (Routledge 2025). His forthcoming book is titled *Exile and Spatiality*.

Bahozde was born in Kirkuk, Iraq into a Kurdish family. At the age of eighteen he escaped Baath-ruled Iraq, and about ten years later he migrated to Canada from Damascus. His Kurdish and Arabic works from his twenties include two books published in Sulaymaniyah and another in Damascus. He holds a PhD in Philosophy from the University of Ottawa (2013). He has designed and taught a wide range of interdisciplinary courses in the social sciences and humanities at several North American universities. He is an associate at Simon Fraser University's Institute of the Humanities.

www.ingramcontent.com/pod-product-compliance
Lightning Source LLC
Chambersburg PA
CBHW071236290326
41931CB00038B/3215